SECRETS
OF THE
ANIMAL WORLD

FISH
Swimming and Floating

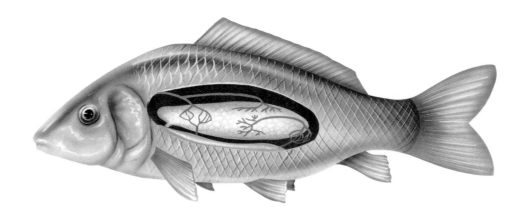

by Isidro Sánchez
Illustrated by Gabriel Casadevall and Ali Garousi

Gareth Stevens Publishing
MILWAUKEE

For a free color catalog describing Gareth Stevens' list of high-quality books and multimedia programs, call 1-800-542-2595 (USA) or 1-800-461-9120 (Canada). Gareth Stevens Publishing's Fax: (414) 225-0377. See our catalog, too, on the World Wide Web: http://gsinc.com

The editor would like to extend special thanks to Jan W. Rafert, Curator of Primates and Small Mammals, Milwaukee County Zoo, Milwaukee, Wisconsin, for his kind and professional help with the information in this book.

Library of Congress Cataloging-in-Publication Data

Sánchez, Isidro.
 [Pez. English]
 Fish: swimming and floating / by Isidro Sánchez; illustrated by Gabriel Casadevall and Ali Garousi.
  p. cm. — (Secrets of the animal world)
 Includes bibliographical references and index.
 Summary: Describes the physical characteristics, habitat, behavior, and life cycle of different kinds of fish.
 ISBN 0-8368-1639-0 (lib. bdg.)
 1. Fishes—Juvenile literature. [1. Fishes.] I. Casadevall, Gabriel, ill. II. Garousi, Ali, ill. III. Title. IV. Series.
 QL617.2.S2613   1997
 597—dc21   96-46933

This North American edition first published in 1997 by
Gareth Stevens Publishing
1555 North RiverCenter Drive, Suite 201
Milwaukee, Wisconsin 53212 USA

This U.S. edition © 1997 by Gareth Stevens, Inc. Created with original © 1993 Ediciones Este, S.A., Barcelona, Spain. Additional end matter © 1997 by Gareth Stevens, Inc.

Series editor: Patricia Lantier-Sampon
Editorial assistants: Diane Laska, Rita Reitci

Printed in the United States of America

1 2 3 4 5 6 7 8 9 01 00 99 98 97

CONTENTS

LIVING IN WATER

The blue planet

Three quarters of our planet is covered in seas and oceans. This is why Earth is sometimes referred to as the blue planet. Millions of fish live in the oceans — as well as in rivers, lakes, and other bodies of water.

A great many fish inhabiting the seas live along coastal areas or in the high seas. Most live close to the water's surface, where sunlight can penetrate.

Many strange and interesting fish species inhabit the ocean depths. Some have luminous dots that help them find food, recognize each other, and frighten enemies in dark waters.

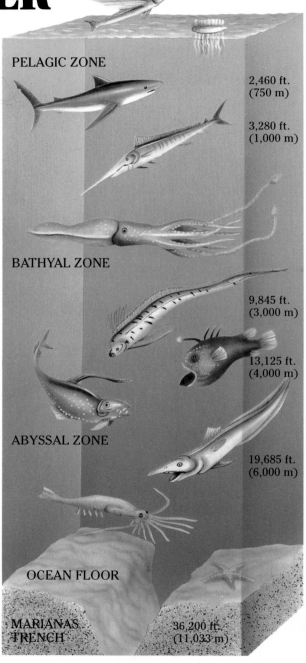

PELAGIC ZONE

2,460 ft. (750 m)

3,280 ft. (1,000 m)

BATHYAL ZONE

9,845 ft. (3,000 m)

13,125 ft. (4,000 m)

ABYSSAL ZONE

19,685 ft. (6,000 m)

OCEAN FLOOR

MARIANAS TRENCH

36,200 ft. (11,033 m)

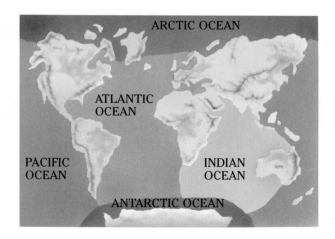

ARCTIC OCEAN

ATLANTIC OCEAN

PACIFIC OCEAN

INDIAN OCEAN

ANTARCTIC OCEAN

There are five oceans in the world (left). The illustration above shows the most common fishes and the depth at which they live.

Float or . . . sink

The largest animals in the world live in the sea. The blue whale, for example, is a giant mammal that can measure 115 feet (35 meters) in length and weigh twenty times more than an African elephant! Yet this incredibly heavy blue whale can float in water. This is possible because sea water is very dense.

Objects float or sink depending on their weight and size. An object's density is its weight divided by its size or volume. Any object less dense than water floats; denser objects sink. A wooden raft, which is less dense than water, floats. A steel screw, denser than water, sinks. Fish float because they are less dense than water.

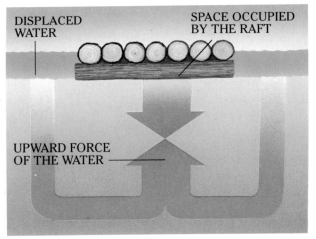

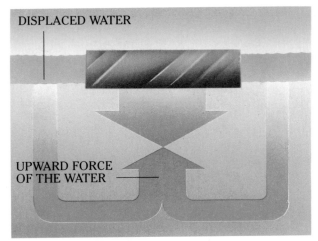

The force of the water toward the surface is equal to the weight of the raft. Therefore, the raft floats.

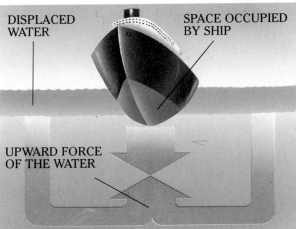

The weight of an iron bar is greater than the upward force of the water. Therefore, the iron bar sinks.

Thanks to the shape of the hull, the upward force of the water supports the ship, so it floats.

Fish species

Fish are vertebrates. This refers to animals that have a spine, such as mammals, amphibians, and birds.

Fish are the most numerous vertebrates, with about 25,000 species. They are grouped into three classes: a) Cyclostomes, a class that includes primitive fishes, such as the lamprey; b) Cartilaginous fish, such as the shark, the ray, and the sawfish; c) Bony fish, the most numerous class, which includes the remaining fishes, such as tunas, sardines, and eels.

Fish come in many shapes and sizes, the most common being a round shape that narrows at both ends to form the tail and head. This streamlined shape enables the fish to swim very fast. Slower fish species

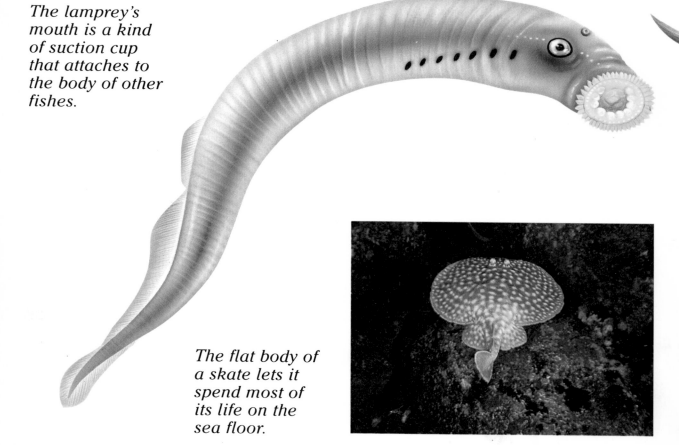

The lamprey's mouth is a kind of suction cup that attaches to the body of other fishes.

The flat body of a skate lets it spend most of its life on the sea floor.

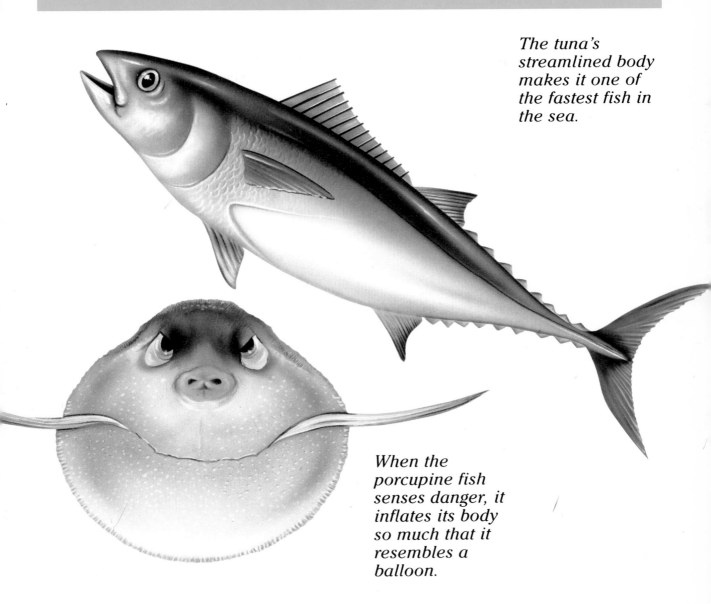

The tuna's streamlined body makes it one of the fastest fish in the sea.

When the porcupine fish senses danger, it inflates its body so much that it resembles a balloon.

rummage around the rocks and seabed. Many of these fish have a "squashed" appearance. This shape lets them rest on the bottom. There are also eel-shaped, arrow-shaped, and balloon-shaped fish. Some have amazing shapes, such as the seahorse and the chimera. Some fish, such as the puffer fish and porcupine fish, can increase their size. When in danger, they swallow air or water to become much larger. In this way they can avoid being swallowed by enemy fish.

INSIDE THE FISH

The fish has adapted perfectly to its watery habitat. It has special organs for breathing under water, and scales and fins that enable it to move swiftly and easily through the water. There are great differences in shape, types of scales, and size of fins.

This illustration shows what the inside of a bony fish, a member of the largest class of fish, looks like.

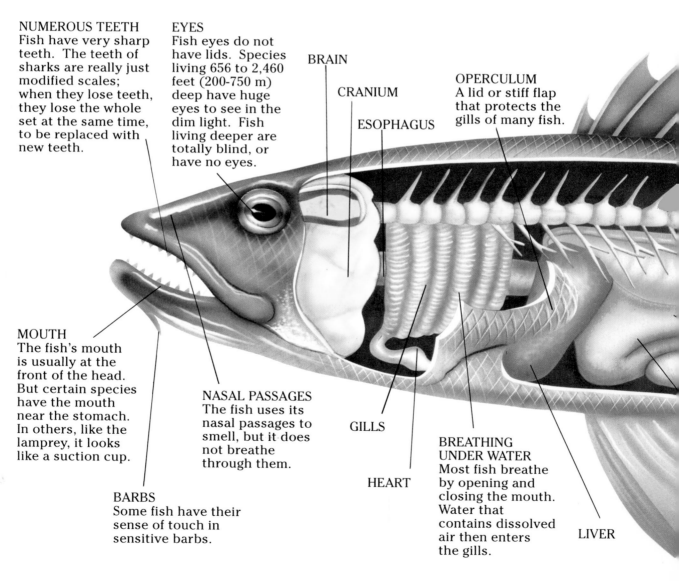

NUMEROUS TEETH
Fish have very sharp teeth. The teeth of sharks are really just modified scales; when they lose teeth, they lose the whole set at the same time, to be replaced with new teeth.

EYES
Fish eyes do not have lids. Species living 656 to 2,460 feet (200-750 m) deep have huge eyes to see in the dim light. Fish living deeper are totally blind, or have no eyes.

BRAIN

CRANIUM

ESOPHAGUS

OPERCULUM
A lid or stiff flap that protects the gills of many fish.

MOUTH
The fish's mouth is usually at the front of the head. But certain species have the mouth near the stomach. In others, like the lamprey, it looks like a suction cup.

NASAL PASSAGES
The fish uses its nasal passages to smell, but it does not breathe through them.

GILLS

HEART

BREATHING UNDER WATER
Most fish breathe by opening and closing the mouth. Water that contains dissolved air then enters the gills.

LIVER

BARBS
Some fish have their sense of touch in sensitive barbs.

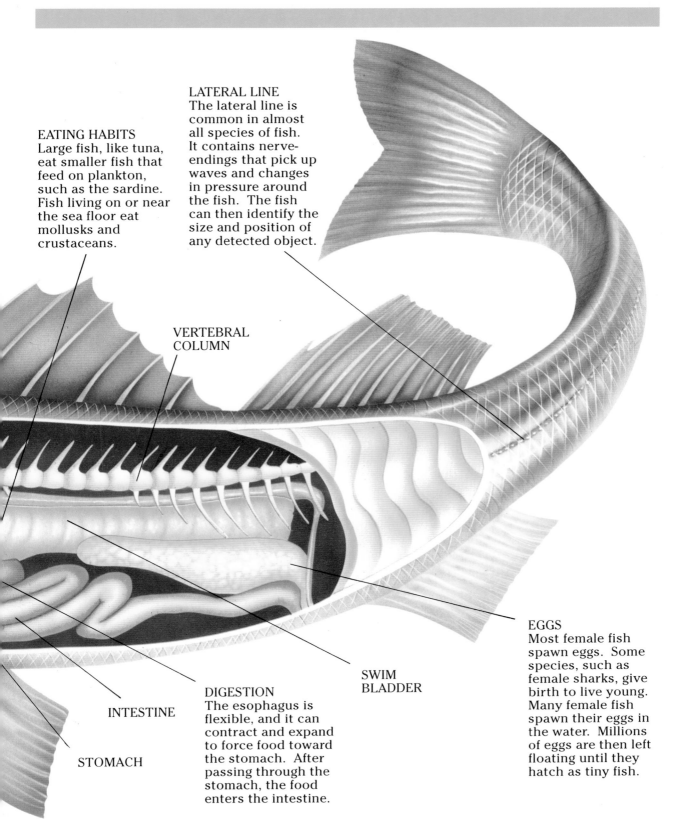

EATING HABITS
Large fish, like tuna, eat smaller fish that feed on plankton, such as the sardine. Fish living on or near the sea floor eat mollusks and crustaceans.

LATERAL LINE
The lateral line is common in almost all species of fish. It contains nerve-endings that pick up waves and changes in pressure around the fish. The fish can then identify the size and position of any detected object.

VERTEBRAL COLUMN

EGGS
Most female fish spawn eggs. Some species, such as female sharks, give birth to live young. Many female fish spawn their eggs in the water. Millions of eggs are then left floating until they hatch as tiny fish.

SWIM BLADDER

INTESTINE

DIGESTION
The esophagus is flexible, and it can contract and expand to force food toward the stomach. After passing through the stomach, the food enters the intestine.

STOMACH

SWIMMING LIKE A FISH

Inflation and deflation

Most bony fish have a swim bladder — a type of pouch containing air that can be inflated and deflated. This allows the fish to move up or down in the water. Some fish in the deepest parts of the oceans do not have a swim bladder. They don't need one because they live a quiet life on or near the sea floor.

In some fish, the bladder is connected to the ear. Changes in water pressure are transmitted by the bladder to the ear, which sends them to the brain as nervous impulses. Fish interpret these signals to determine a proper swimming depth.

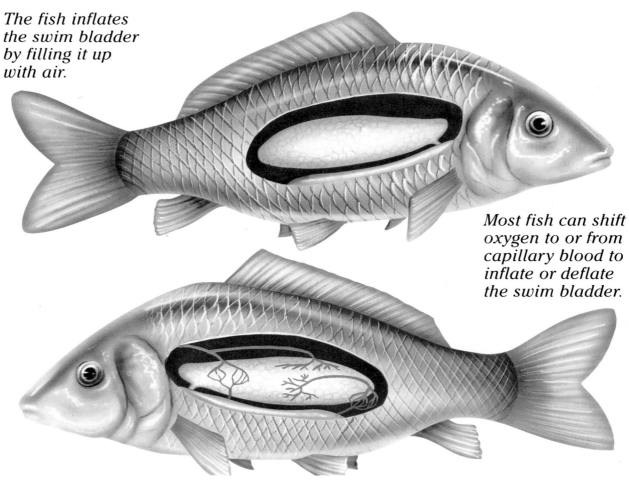

The fish inflates the swim bladder by filling it up with air.

Most fish can shift oxygen to or from capillary blood to inflate or deflate the swim bladder.

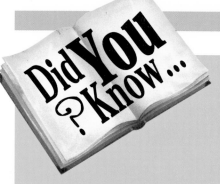

that there are horses in the sea?

The seahorse has a very unusual appearance. Its body is totally different from other fishes and resembles a knight in a game of chess. It swims upright and propels itself with a dorsal fin, which moves like a small propeller.

To reproduce, the female seahorse lays eggs in a brood pouch on the front of the male, who then cares for them. After four weeks, the eggs hatch, and the baby seahorses are released into the sea.

An adaptable float

The swim bladder acts like a float that fish can inflate or deflate with air. This enables the fish to remain afloat while not moving. It also helps the fish move up or down.

Without the swim bladder, a fish would have to keep moving to keep itself from sinking, as is the case with sharks. When a fish sinks, the swim bladder deflates because there is more pressure underneath than on the surface. The fish then inflates

The shark moves its caudal fin (1) to the right and left. The dorsal fin (2) acts like a rudder. The pectoral fins (3) stabilize the fish.

the bladder to be able to float under water.

When the fish goes to the surface, the opposite happens.

Near the surface, the swim bladder adopts the necessary size to float. As the fish descends, the swim

bladder becomes smaller because the pressure is greater. So air moves in from nearby capillaries to inflate it.

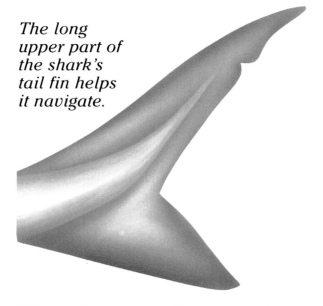

The long upper part of the shark's tail fin helps it navigate.

of air in the bladder. Fishermen often catch fish as inflated as balloons because they had no time to empty the air from their swim bladders.

The shark does not have a swim bladder, so it never stops swimming. The upper end of the caudal fin is much longer than the lower. This helps the shark stay afloat while swimming. The special shape of its pectoral fins also prevents it from sinking, since they act like stabilizers.

The fish is going from one depth where the water pressure is great to another where there is less pressure. The bladder inflates, and the fish expels the excess air. It rises slowly and gradually reduces the amount

As the fish swims toward the surface, the bladder increases in size. The fish gradually releases the air inside.

BORN TO SWIM

Fins, the fish's arms and legs

The fish's fins allow it to live and move around in the water, and help make it a champion swimmer. The fish uses its fins to propel and stabilize itself in the water, and also as rudders for changing direction. The fins are composed of thin bones lightly covered with skin.

The fins have different names depending on where they are. The dorsal fin is on the back.

The fin's many bones are placed in front of one another.

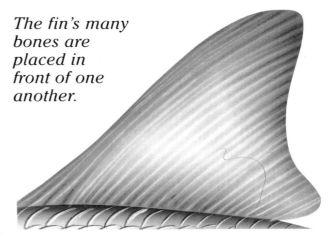

The pectoral and pelvic fins are on the abdomen. The anal fin is at the end of the fish's underside, and the caudal fin is commonly known as a fish tail.

The catfish lives in calm waters, such as slow-moving rivers and lakes. It has a ferocious appetite and eats all kinds of small prey.

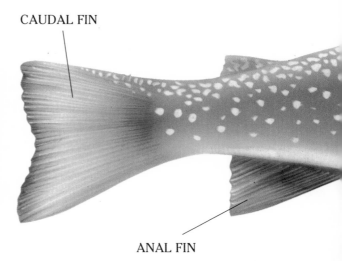

CAUDAL FIN

ANAL FIN

Some fins come in pairs. Most fish have only one dorsal fin, one anal fin, and one caudal fin.

All fish, however, have two pectoral and two pelvic fins. Situated one on each side of the fish, these fins correspond to a human's arms and legs.

Pelvic fins are smaller than pectorals. Some species of fish, especially those that live deep down in the ocean, have very long pectoral fins. They may protrude in disc or rhombus shapes, which the fish use to rest on the sea bottom.

Many colored fish have large fins that are used more for attracting the opposite sex than for swimming.

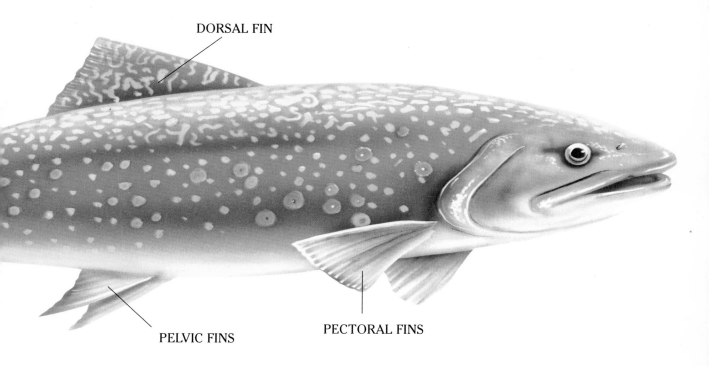

DORSAL FIN

PELVIC FINS

PECTORAL FINS

that there are "cleaner" fish?

"Cleaner" fish actually clean the skin of other fish species. The cleaners eat parasites that they extract from their customers. Any fish that needs a clean-up simply approaches the cleaner fish and lets them get to work.

The small cleaner fish enter the gills of the larger fish to begin their task or examine the outside fins to see what must be done.

Even the ferocious shark permits these tiny fish to move around its teeth, looking for debris.

Propulsion

Certain fish species, such as the eel, swim by making wavy movements with their bodies. Others, like the ray, move the fins on their abdomen.

The best swimmers, such as swordfish and flying fish, propel themselves through the water by rapid movements of their caudal fins. The turbulence produced by these movements propels them forward at high speed. Their streamlined bodies also help them swim fast.

A fish's speed in the water is closely related to its length. Long fishes with small caudal fins can reach speeds of over 25 miles (40 km) an hour. The

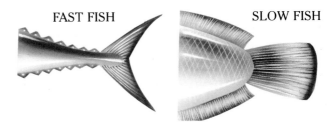

FAST FISH   SLOW FISH

A speedy fish's caudal fin has a shape different from that of a slow fish.

The eel swims by wriggling its body. This is easy because of its body's long, cylindrical shape.

fastest fish in the world is the swordfish, which can swim up to 80 miles (130 km) an hour.

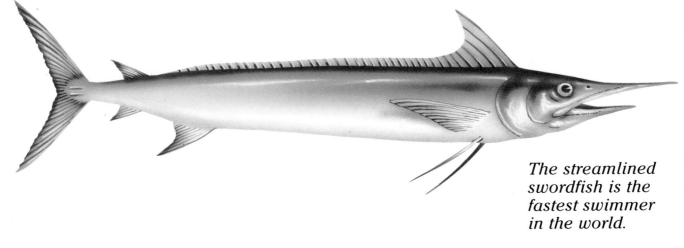

The streamlined swordfish is the fastest swimmer in the world.

Navigation instruments

The caudal fin helps propel the fish forward, but the other fins are used for navigating — turning, braking, or reversing. The dorsal and anal fins are the fish's rudders. They enable it to set a course and change direction.

The fins of this lion fish are its defensive weapons.

The abdominal fins are brakes and stabilizers. By spreading these fins, the fish can create more resistance and slow down or stop. If it moves these fins in the opposite direction, the fish can swim backward or tread water. When using the fins as stabilizers, the fish can make turns by extending the fin on one side of its body more than the other. Fish can also use their fins for defense or even as wings.

The dorsal fin (1) is the fish's rudder.

By folding the other fins (2), the fish can go up and down in the water.

that the archerfish has an excellent aim?

The river-dwelling archerfish catches prey by squirting water at it with amazing accuracy. It can catch insects that rest on leaves or plant stems from a distance up to 6.5 feet (2 m). The archerfish swims to the surface and sticks a small part of its mouth out of the water. It fills its mouth with water and turns its tongue into a tube, which it then uses to spit out the water.

FISH ANCESTORS

Armored fish

Life on Earth began in the sea, originating from primitive algae. The first vertebrates also appeared in the sea about 500 million years ago. They were small species of fish, without jaws or fins.

In time, these fish developed fins on the back and abdomen, and their bodies were covered by bony, armor-plated shields. About 450 million years ago, fish developed jaws and teeth. They became predators, so they needed to swim fast to catch prey. Gradually, they developed other fins for this purpose.

Anglaspio, a prehistoric fish, lived about 450 million years ago.

Many fish ancestors had a hard, bony covering. The coelacanth still possesses this protective shield.

PINICHTYS

COELACANTH

Great reptiles of the sea

About 250 million years ago, when dinosaurs dominated Earth, some large reptiles lived in the sea. The plesiosaurs fed on squid and small species of fish. They had enormous fins for swimming, very similar to today's turtles. They also had a long neck to search for prey in the water.

Many prehistoric fish had lungs; they breathed air above the water's surface. At that time, Earth had very damp periods or very dry ones. In damp periods, fish used their gills to breathe. But the waters stagnated in dry times, and the fish survived only because they had lungs. Today, only a few fish have lungs; they are known as Dipnoi or lung fish.

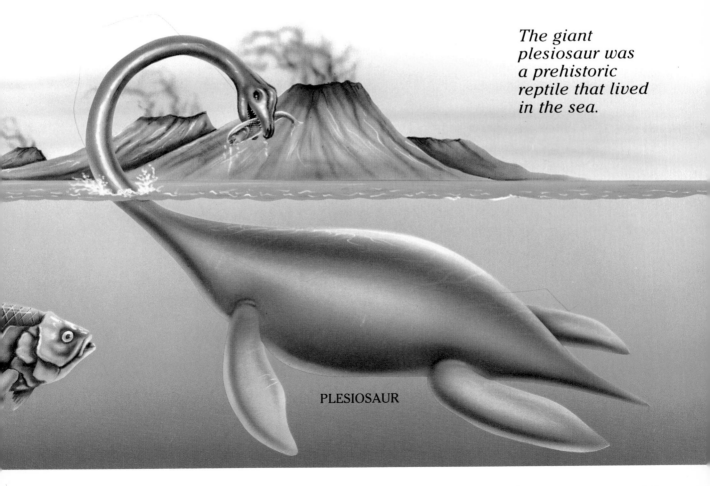

The giant plesiosaur was a prehistoric reptile that lived in the sea.

PLESIOSAUR

STEEL GIANTS

Ships with fins

Ships move by the action of the propeller, very much like a fish's caudal fin. As the propeller turns, a huge amount of water is displaced. Response to this movement drives the ship.

The ship's rudder works the same way as a fish's other fins. It makes the ship turn. Despite the fact that humans have imitated the fish's propulsion mechanisms, the great ships of the sea are not as fast. These steel giants travel only at about 15 or 20 knots an hour — the equivalent of less than 25 miles (40 km) an hour. Speedboats, however, can travel over 125 miles (200 km) an hour.

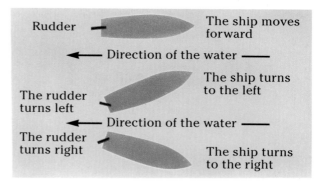

The propeller pushes the water back

Direction of the water

HOW A SHIP'S PROPELLER WORKS

The propeller's action produces a reaction in the water that propels the ship forward

HOW A SHIP'S RUDDER WORKS

Rudder

The ship moves forward

Direction of the water

The rudder turns left

The ship turns to the left

Direction of the water

The rudder turns right

The ship turns to the right

The hull of a ship and the position of its propellers and rudder.

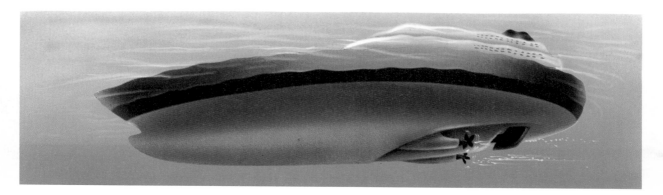

Submarine: a fish in water

A fish and a submarine use similar systems for submerging and surfacing. But there are differences, too.

When a fish submerges, it inflates its swim bladder. To surface, it deflates the swim bladder. A submarine has enormous tanks along the hull. When these tanks are full of air, the submarine floats. When the tanks are filled with water, the submarine submerges.

Bathyspheres hold the record for deep sea diving: 36,200 feet (11,033 m) in the Pacific Ocean's Marianas trench.

When the submarine travels under water, it moves like a fish, turning and moving backward. It also has several rudders to help it change course.

A submarine floats when its tanks are filled with air.

To dive, the submarine floods its tanks with water. It moves by balancing the amount of water.

To surface, the submarine replaces the water in its tanks with compressed air.

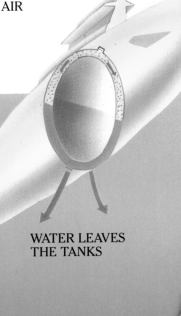

COMPRESSED AIR

AIR

WATER ENTERS THE TANKS

HULL

TANKS

WATER LEAVES THE TANKS

APPENDIX TO

SECRETS
OF THE
ANIMAL WORLD

FISH
Swimming and Floating

FISH SECRETS

▼ **The longest fish.** The longest fish in the world is the whale shark, which measures 56 feet (17 m) in length.

Millions of eggs floating in the sea. The moon fish spawns the largest number of eggs — over 300 million total.

▼ **"Fishing" with a line.** The angler fish attracts its prey with a kind of fishing line that hangs out in front of its mouth. Any fish that becomes too curious about it ends up in the angler's ferocious mouth.

Enormous Fins. The manta ray has enormous fins that measure over 20 feet (6 m) from one end to the other.

▼ **A powerful sword.** The swordfish has a spike at the end of its snout that can measure as long as 5 feet (1.5 m).

A long childhood. The baby conger eel takes a long time to grow up. It floats around in the sea for one or two years before becoming an adult.

A fish that walks. The walking fish of southeast Asia can travel over land. When its lake dries up, it can "walk" long distances to another lake.

▼ A wonder of nature. Coral reefs are enormous colonies of tiny organisms that look like flowers and small trees. The largest coral reef in the world is the Great Barrier Reef, off the Australian coast. It is 730 miles (1,170 km) long and can be seen from as far away as the moon.

▲ A great kisser. The gourami kisser gets its name from its ritual fights, in which it kisses its opponent.

1. How many species of fish are there?
a) 325.
b) About 25,000.
c) 1,000,000.

2. What are gills?
a) Organs for breathing.
b) Barbs on a fish's snout.
c) Several holes in a tail.

3. What is a swim bladder?
a) A fish's stomach.
b) An organ that enables a fish to float.
c) A pouch where young are born.

4. Does the shark have a swim bladder?
a) Yes.
b) No.
c) It has one, but does not need it.

5 A seahorse's eggs develop:
a) in a nest on the sea floor.
b) in deep water after the female abandons them.
c) in a pouch on the male's front.

6. A fish uses its caudal fin to:
a) propel it forward.
b) provide it with oxygen.
c) clean its scales.

The answers to FISH SECRETS questions are on page 32.

GLOSSARY

abdomen: the section of an animal's body that contains the digestive organs.

adapt: to make changes or adjustments in order to survive in a changing environment.

algae: a simple plant that lives in the sea, one of the earliest forms of life on Earth.

amphibians: cold-blooded animals that live both in water and on land. Frogs, toads, and salamanders are amphibians.

anal: referring to the area of an organism's anus, the opening through which wastes are expelled. The anal fin of fish is near the anus.

barb: a sharp point that sticks out backward.

capillaries: tiny blood vessels that connect veins to arteries.

caudal: the fin at a fish's tail that adds speed and thrust to the fish's propulsion.

contract (*v*): to pull in and make smaller, shorter, or tighter.

crustaceans: animals with segmented bodies and a hard outer shell that live mostly in water. Lobsters, shrimp, and crabs are crustaceans.

debris: the scattered remains of something that has been broken or destroyed.

deflate: to release air or gas from.

dense: having parts packed closely together.

dorsal: referring to the back, or topmost, part of an organ or an animal in its normal position; i.e., a fish has a dorsal fin.

esophagus: the tube inside the body that connects the throat to the stomach so food can pass into it.

flexible: able to bend or move with ease.

float: to be held up, or sustained, at the water's surface.

gills: the breathing organs in all fish. Gills are also known as the branchiae.

habitat: the natural home of a plant or animal.

hull: the body or frame of a ship that includes only its sides and bottom areas.

inflate: to fill with air or gas and expand.

inhabit: to live in or on.

lateral lines: sensory organs that run along the sides of fish. These help the fish detect motion and vibration in the water.

luminous: shining; giving off light.

mammals: warm-blooded animals that have backbones, hair, and that give live birth. Female mammals produce milk to feed their young.

mollusks: invertebrate animals, such as snails and clams, that usually live in water and have hard outer shells.

navigate: to direct the course of a boat, plane, or craft of some sort.

operculum: a stiff lid or covering flap.

parasite: a plant or animal that lives on another plant or animal and gets its food from that plant or animal, called a host.

pectoral: (fins) that extend from the side of the animal's body. They help guide the fish up and down.

plankton: tiny plants and animals that drift in the ocean and feed whales and other sea animals.

predators: animals that kill and eat other animals.

prey: animals that are hunted and killed for food by other animals.

primitive: of or relating to an early and usually simple stage of development.

propel: to move in a forward direction.

reptiles: a group of cold-blooded animals that have backbones, crawl on the ground, and have scaly skin.

rhombus: a geometric figure with four equal sides, especially without right angles.

rudder: a movable board or plate mounted at the rear end of a boat to help in steering.

rummage: to search thoroughly.

scales: small, thin, platelike pieces that overlap to cover fish and reptiles.

snout: protruding nose and jaw of an animal.

spawn: to lay eggs and reproduce.

species: animals or plants that are closely related and often similar in behavior and appearance. Members of the same species can breed together.

stabilizer: a structure, like a fin, that prevents excessive rolling.

stagnate: to remain motionless, without current.

submerge: to go beneath the water; to cover with water.

turbulence: irregular motion in air or water with strong up and down currents.

vertebrates: animals that have backbones and internal skeletons.

ACTIVITIES

◆ The ocean supplies large amounts of nourishing food for humans. Pollution and overfishing are two activities that can affect this supply of food. Do some research to find out how ocean pollution affects this valuable source of food. What can we do to prevent or overcome this pollution? Some other kinds of food from the sea are shelled animals, crustaceans, and mammals. Does the pollution that affects fish also affect these food resources? Should we allow unlimited fishing? Why or why not? What can we do to preserve these important stocks of food?

◆ Scientists often need to go into the ocean depths in order to study fish and other sea life. Design your own deep-sea research vessel, using library books and magazines, such as *National Geographic*, that describe these submersibles. Draw diagrams to show how your vessel would provide light, warmth, and air for the occupants, a way to collect specimens, and lights to explore the ocean depths. Draw some imaginary creatures that your scientists might discover.

MORE BOOKS TO READ

Amazing Fish. Mary Ling (Knopf Books for Young Readers)
Dangerous Fish. Ray Broekel (Childrens)
Extremely Weird Fish. Sara Lovett (John Muir)
Fish. Donna Baily (Raintree Steck-Vaughn)
Fish. Edward Ricciuti (Blackbirch)
Fish Do the Strangest Things. John F. Eggert (Random Books
    for Young Readers)
Fishes. B. Armstrong (Learning Works)
Surprising Swimmers. Anthony D. Fredericks (NorthWord)
Those Amazing Eels. Cheryl M. Halton (Silver Burdett)

VIDEOS

Fish. (Agency for Instructional Technology)
Fish. (AIMS Media)
Fish Are Interesting. (Phoenix/BFA Films and Video)
Fish: A First Inquiry. (Phoenix/BFA Films and Video)
The Fish Embryo: From Fertilization to Hatching. (Encyclopædia
    Britannica Educational Corp.)

PLACES TO VISIT

Indianapolis Zoo
In White River State Park
1200 W. Washington Street
Indianapolis, IN 46222

The Aquarium
Marine Parade
Napier, New Zealand

Sea World
7007 Sea World Drive
Orlando, FL 32821

Taronga Zoo
Bradley's Head Road
Mosman, NSW
Australia 2088

Aquarium du Quebec
1675 Avenue des Hotels
Sainte-Foy, PQ G1W 4S3

New York Aquarium
W. 8th St. and Surf Ave.
Brooklyn, NY 11224

**Vancouver Public
  Aquarium**
In Stanley Park
West Georgia Avenue
Vancouver, BC V6B 3X8

**Sea World on the Gold
  Coast**
Sea World Drive Spit
Surfers Paradise
Queensland, Australia
4217

INDEX

Answers to FISH SECRETS questions:

1. b
2. a
3. b
4. b
5. c
6. a